Antony Hollingsworth was born and raised within the countryside of North Wales where he spent his childhood playing with his friends and younger brothers on Halkyn mountain and the surrounding rivers and hills. He also helped out on the family's small holding and spending the best part of his working life in the local authority as a road worker while struggling with depression for a number of years. He found himself writing little poems about nature and his depression on scraps of paper. Then one day, his girlfriend read them and gave him a notebook and said, write your thoughts in here. Almost a decade later, numerous notebooks were filled with poems. He has decided to share with the world what he has gone through, with poems about his daily struggles and moments of joy and happiness. Nowadays, when his depression permits him, he writes poetry and spends his time walking up mountains and within nature to help him reflect on life.

Anthony Hollingsworth

MOMENTS OF JOY – MOMENTS OF DARKNESS

AUSTIN MACAULEY PUBLISHERS™
LONDON • CAMBRIDGE • NEW YORK • SHARJAH

Copyright © Anthony Hollingsworth 2023

The right of Anthony Hollingsworth to be identified as author of this work has been asserted by the author in accordance with sections 77 and 78 of the Copyright, Designs and Patents Act 1988.

All rights reserved. No part of this publication may be reproduced, stored in a retrieval system, or transmitted in any form or by any means, electronic, mechanical, photocopying, recording, or otherwise, without the prior permission of the publishers.

Any person who commits any unauthorised act in relation to this publication may be liable to criminal prosecution and civil claims for damages.

A CIP catalogue record for this title is available from the British Library.

ISBN 9781398450042 (Paperback)
ISBN 9781398455252 (Hardback)
ISBN 9781398455269 (ePub e-book)

www.austinmacauley.com

First Published 2023
Austin Macauley Publishers Ltd®
1 Canada Square
Canary Wharf
London
E14 5AA

Table of Contents

A White Dream	7
A Winters' Moment	8
Awakening	9
Birth	10
Black Dog	11
Close of Day	13
Courtship	14
Cut	16
Deepest Blackness	18
Depression	19
Drowsing	20
Feeling Happy	21
Human Life?	22
In the Light	23
Its Name	24
Lost Within	26

Lost Loved Ones	27
Lullaby Lie Down	28
Mirrored	30
Mountain	31
My Everything	33
Mysterious Journey	35
Not Again	37
Not Living Only Hiding	38
Out of Fuel	40
Peaceful Time	41
Princess	42
Quiet Contemplation	44
Shaft of Light	45
Snow Drop	47
Step Forward	49
The Wild Wood	50
Thunderstorm	52
Tick Tock	53
Together	54
Tree	55
Valentine	56
Will Power	57
Winters' Morn	59

A White Dream

Life,
Where to begin?
Life,
What does it mean?
Lying here the buzzer is on,
But my eyes stay shut,
I don't want to get up,
Shut up will you buzzing by my head,
I want to sleep I want to forget,
I dream a dream –
A dream so white –
A dream so clean,
But a black dirty life keeps
It keeps tugging at me,
Get up…wake up your life awaits you,
Your dreams are not real,
The buzzer continues…

A Winters' Moment

I strain my eyes to the mountain yonder,
A beam of light pushes through the blackness
Onto the snow-capped mountains…
My thoughts stand still,
My mind is captured,
By the sight, I see
The mountains yonder.

Awakening

Dawn rises out of the murky night,
The hazy grey a welcome sight,
A beam of light breaks through the gloom,
You see your day unfold before you –
A brew in one hand,
Toast in the other…
A deep breath rushes into your lungs
As your body awakens with the morning songs…
The sun rises beyond the hill,
A bird sings out with the cockerels doodle doo,
The chill retreating, the shadows departing,
This day has dawned,
A new beginning
On this day of reckoning…
I will not fail you.

Birth

From that moment a miracle,
Life has more meaning,
A smile keeps getting wider
Growing into a grin,
A lot of noise
But only one thing you hear,
The sound to tell you
That life will now begin.

Black Dog

Go into the mist,
It will hide you, protect you
From the Black dogs,
You their prey,
They howl
Trying to find you,
Not able to pick up your scent,
But still fresh are the scars
Of past battles –
Not always won,
But here in the mist,
You can regroup your thoughts,
Have a rest,
The Black dogs
Live only off your fear,
So be calm,
Let your mind be at peace,
So sit tight,
But be strong
Without fear,
Or the dogs will devour you –
Fear by tear,

The mist will hide you
But not forever,
You have to fight them,
Face that fear,
So do it now –
Bite back!
Hear them yelping,
See them running –
Their howls disappear,
Not all at once
But one by one,
They will give up,
Leave you be
That is when the mist lift,
When it will be clear
And you are at peace,
You have no fear.

Close of Day

I hope I wake as happy as I sleep.
I hope I wake with a spring in my step.
For tomorrow is a new day
And today has been great…
But tomorrow that new day anticipated,
It comes with joy
But also with dread.
For each day is different,
That is the trouble –
Not knowing
How I will wake up
From a night's slumber,
Shall it be with a spring in my step?
Or a chain around my neck?
That is a worry,
The dread
At the close of day –
For night time sometimes my savoir,
The new day –
Sometimes my pain.

Courtship

I dance,
I prance,
I preen,
Trying to attract my queen,
A hedgerow,
A wall,
A playground,
A yard,
These are my stages,
For this grand visage
With a puffed out breast,
A tail held high,
I dance,
I prance,
As I sing my serenade,
My tail held high,
She has a look,
She whizzes past by,
Maybe I'm in luck,
I hope I won't cry,
Yes she is back,
This time a slower flyby,

She must be interested,
Best lift my tail towards the sky,
A few little dance moves,
Why not…it's worth a try,
She stops, tilts her head
Looking oh so fine,
I think I have found my queen,
The live of my life
With a twitch of her wings,
She is by my side,
No more to be said,
Just a bob of the head,
She is my queen,
What a find…|!

Cut

Snip
Snip
Snip
The noise their tools make,
Carnage covers the floor,
Lives being trodden on,
Cut short
Before their prime,
Snip
Snip
Snip
Will it ever end?
Short,
Long,
Coloured,
Curled,
It does not matter
To the butcher's trade –
Tools so sharp
That the very air is not safe,
A fingered stick,
Parts loved ones embraced,

Knotted they thought forever,
Then snip,
They fall to die,
Fallen,
Trodden,
Amongst the sea of hair.

Deepest Blackness

Deep
Down,
Where the dark things lay,
A blackness deeper
Than the nights sky,
Hidden away
From eyes searching
And things lurking,
Eyes so large,
Or none –
Blind to it all,
Endlessly wondering
In a gloomy blackness,
No light
To guide them
In this deepest blackness.

Depression

I am here,
I am now,
So many things to see around me,
But the void that is in front of me
Is all that I can see…
It's endless and timeless –
Trapping me,
Sometimes, I glimpse another world –
A softer quieter world,
I reach out,
I touch it,
A warm glow surrounds me,
I am there where I was,
Happy,
Everyone around me is smiling,
Patting me on the back,
Is it all over has the void gone?
No…
It whispers
Quietly,
No…
I am not gone.

Drowsing

Lie down a deep breath,
Then a sigh…
Close your eyes for a bit,
Another deep breath,
Another long sigh,
Your eyes open for a bit,
One last look around
Before saying goodnight,
A yawn and a smile,
So,
It's goodnight for today,
We start afresh tomorrow –
A new beginning…a new day.

Feeling Happy

It may be dull,
It may be windy,
Outside is cold,
But inside I am warming,
My heart is awoken,
A joy to be living,
A life worth having…

Human Life?

It's all about life the world we live in,
It surrounds us…consumes us…we hold it in,
So scared we might lose it but think nothing of taking it from others.

In the Light

Light, time, darkness,
They go hand in hand, whether we like it or not,
Try your best to live life in the light…
Let darkness take care of itself,
Light is your friend,
It will take care of you,
Provide –
Nurture you,
Stand barefoot in the grass,
Wiggle your toes,
Hold your arms out wide,
Close your eyes,
Breathe deeply what nature provides.

Its Name

Want…
The thing we chase,
The thing we need,
But want is an elusive thing;
It jumps within our grasp
Just to jump back again,
It taunts us,
We chase it,
We seek it here and there,
Sometimes we catch it
But it just makes us want more,
So, like a dog chasing its tail,
We chase it once more.
But one day,
Something else rushes by you,
No wait it is you who rushes past it –
A thing unfamiliar –
But you smile not knowing why all the same,
Want stops pulling at your senses,
As you look at it again,
But your mind is wondering,
What this strange thing is?

And a new feeling course through your veins –
Unusual and strange –
Wait I know what this is,
I know its name,
A feeling we once knew is here again,
Then your smile widens
Turning into a grin,
The thing that stops you…
Rushing chasing and wanting,
Love and passion is its name.

Lost Within

Blackness…
So deep so grim,
It surrounds from without
And from within,
So long I have spent here,
It feels like home it feels safe
But I know I am trapped,
Sealed within…
Blackness is
Everywhere.
Light is pushed out
And cannot get back in,
I shout
But there is no echo,
Sound does not know
Where to begin,
So, sit still,
Be quiet,
The blackness
Has begun to win.

Lost Loved Ones

A moment has passed,
And grief is here…
A soul has passed on,
Its peace is real…
Its peace is tranquil,
A life faded but never forgotten,
In our memories they stay – their lives eternal,
Time moves on griefs grip its lessons,
Our souls mend – our lives continue,
So come take a pew,
Sit with me…be merry,
For time is a healer,
Our
Memories
Are plenty.

Lullaby Lie Down

A sudden gust blow in,
The clouds moving faster,
The grass around me
Swaying,
There must be a storm somewhere
But not here,
Above the clouds
Is the blue sky,
High above that
The sun beams down,
As I lie in the grass,
The world going by –
The gust evaporates,
A breeze now in its stead,
The sun
Shining down,
It's a good time
For a lazy lie down,
With a gentle breeze
Blowing over me,
There is hardly a sound,
A quiet moment, turns into

A lengthy lullaby,
Moves on
Without hardly a notice
Of me lying here quietly.

Mirrored

Look at your reflection,
Looking back at you –
Those eyes staring
Deep into your soul,
It shows you how you feel,
Every line
On your face,
A story…
A memory lived…
Look at yourself,
As your reflection looks inward.

Mountain

A clear view
Of your surroundings around you,
Standing tall and rugged,
A king among men
Watching over Dale and Glen,
The lakeside below you
Tickling at your toes,
While the clouds above you,
Say hello,
You are magnificent,
A splendour to all
Clouds shadows,
Painting pictures across you,
As they pass by
Saying hello,
Sometimes the clouds come down
To make music with you –
Noise and light –
Its chorus echoing
Through the Dale and Glen,
And after the party,
They cry joyous

Or maybe sorrow,
Their tears
Running down you
To the lake below
Stand tall,
Stand proud,
Protecting your land
For you are a mountain,
Above all others you stand.

My Everything

I curse the thoughts going around in my head,
They do not feel like mine,
I don't normally think like this,
Dark thoughts,
There are so many,
They push out
Anything –
Everything good
I once thought I held dear,
Filling me with blackness,
Filling me with doubt,
My head rests on my arm
Leaning on the writing desk –
The writing desk I call home,
My face
Hidden from a world of pain,
Snap
The lead breaks,
As I push too hard
Without thinking,
These dark thoughts
Keep going around

Inside my head –
I feel the goodness,
My own thoughts
Seeping out of me,
To disappear
Into nothingness,
Into blackness taking over,
My mind,
My soul,
My everything…

Mysterious Journey

Cometh the daytime me now,
I tread footsteps
Of a thousand and more,
Scenes strange to me,
But to others are normal,
Wonderful creations
Once new are now old,
My feet follow others,
I gaze at many wondrous things,
But as always,
It's the structure of things,
From the table leg
To the door hinge,
That intrigue me,
Wonderful stonework
Laid with passion,
Skill,
It keeps it all hidden,
Keeps it all well,
Passion,
Happiness,
Sorrow,

Raised voices in laughter, anger,
Lives living within the walls, in and out,
I visit the ale House,
A packet of crisps,
A pint of the best,
A little table,
A cushion by the window,
My journey continues…
Those thousand steps and more,
Scenes that get darker,
More mysterious,
On the way home,
A fallen tree,
A broken gate,
An owl hoots,
So,
My journey ends,
Ends like countless
Before me…

Not Again

It gnaws,
It gnaws,
I feel it getting stronger…
Bubbling,
Rising,
An impossible feeling,
Ready to blow,
I try to hold it at bay
But at bait will not stay,
For soon,
It will win –
Win –
Break through my depression,
Raise its ugly head,
It scares me,
Scares the life out of me,
Knowing I am not strong enough
To win.

Not Living Only Hiding

I have wasted my life
Wishing I was someone else –
Not a different life,
Just a different me,
My life seems so wasted
Wishing I was him,
Not being contented with me,
So here lie
On this lounger,
Watching the world flow by,
Wishing I was him,
Is everyone around me content?
Or do they wish too?
To be a different them…
Time is flowing,
Like the water around me,
And so a thought comes to me,
The water around me it is the same
Weather it flows or is still,
It does not wish to be
The sun or the moon,
It is just happy being water,

Either still or moving,
So my thoughts change
A little like the water,
Turning into a ripple
Gently lapping
Against my mind,
It is a wonder,
This world we live in,
This life of mine,
For so long it has been this way,
For I must have maybe spent
Half this life of mine
Wanting to be him,
I want to spend my other half
Being me –
And not him –
As I think this,
The bubbles rise,
The clouds roll by,
The sun comes out and shines,
I hope this life of mine will change…
Sometimes being still,
Sometimes a ripple
Or a torrent,
But as me, not as him in disguise.

Out of Fuel

O dear not again,
A sigh a shake of the head,
Not again…
An embarrassed look on your face
As it goes red,
You phone your dad up,
Yes,
I have done it again,
That little light is flashing,
The dial has hit that empty mark,
Yes it's on red,
Your dad turns up
And just shakes his head,
Muttering typical –
Yet again.

Peaceful Time

It is peaceful and cool,
The breeze is gentle,
The trees talk and leaves sing,
A chorus cries out from the birds in the sky,
This quiet spot,
Full of wonder,
Lying under the trees
Amongst the fallen leaves,
Listening…
Listening…
Listening…

Princess

Golden was the sun
That shone down its warming light,
Your fair hair
Glinting,
Smelling
Like new daisies,
On a beautiful crisp spring day,
You walk through the woods
With a skip in your stride,
You smile
And the trees seem to wave their arms in joy
At your happiness this day,
Pink and white blossom
Float around your feet
As you skip along
The woodland path,
Giving a glimpse of
What it would look like
If you walked among the clouds in the sky,
You twirl your dress follows,
And I am sure angles sing,
The rabbits and squirrels,

The birds and the bees,
All stop what they are doing –
Watching you go on your way –
Their princess,
Their queen,
Nature in harmony,
The land, the sky and the sea…

Quiet Contemplation

For here I sit upon my throne
Where so many decisions are made,
But the same outcome remains,
Reading the news
From around this kingdom,
From far and from wide,
Of battles won
And of battles lost,
Sometimes a happy story
Comes my way,
And this throne I sit upon
Seems worth keeping
For one more day –
A lifetime sat here,
A lifetime to come…

Shaft of Light

A shaft of light
Breaks free of the clouds,
Quickly engulfing
The small village below,
The light knows
Its time is short,
For soon the clouds
Will enshroud it,
Once more,
It seeks out
All the nooks and crannies,
The hidden corners
Where shadows can hide,
It shouts out to every
Man, woman and child,
And animal –
Come stand outside,
Look to where I come from,
I am the light
That keeps the dark at bay,
Warms your skin
And lights up the day,

I'm not here for long –
A light so strong –
But all too short
For the clouds
Are out –
Playing today too.

Snow Drop

It is a year's rest I have had
Hibernating away –
Until the winter winds calm,
I start to squirm and stretch
My way out of cocoon,
Poking my head out
To see if the coast is clear,
Then a little more…
Soon I am free,
A little closer to the sun
I put my white hat on,
My face opens to the world,
O, it is good to be free again
In this winter's sun,
All my neighbours
Are doing the same,
Nodding hello
To one and all,
The snow has gone…
But a new carpet of white
Covers the land,
The start of new life

On this new spring dawn…
We are only here
For a little while,
We hope our smiles
Make you smile too,
But we must go soon –
O slumber –
To hibernate away,
For next year
Is not far away,
Then we will
See each other
Once again…

Step Forward

Every footstep is a new step
On the journey of life,
No matter
Where each footstep falls,
It is new
And has potential
To move the world around you,
Every footstep takes you forward
Not backward,
So, follow them forward
To the future,
Not backward to the past…
Leave that behind you
Where it belongs.

The Wild Wood

It creaks,
It groans,
Chatting away
So many voices with something to say,
But listen they all do,
Listen all day,
They consume their comrades,
Their fallen friends,
Their life ended
Seeps into them,
So that theirs never ends
Other lives live around them,
All in harmony –
Their bodies to be consumed
When they come to an end,
A change comes upon them,
A time to show off
All their wonder and splendour
Before it all drops off,
The wonder and magic of colours –
Of odours coming together
That only nature can provide,

Then one day,
It is over
With a rustle and a shudder,
It is time to go quiet…
Time to slumber
For winter is coming.

Thunderstorm

The light doth dwindle the darkness creeps in,
The wind is blowing –
A rage is blowing,
BOOM is the noise we fear,
CRACK is the light so clear,
The wind is howling…the trees are groaning,
BOOM again the darkness is deeper,
A few drops to start with,
A storm, it is here!

Tick Tock

What time is it?
Time – where is it?
Sitting alone or sharing,
Time is wanting,
Needing,
Suffocating,
No watch no clock,
But still
It ticks by,
Tick tock…
Why won't it stop?
How long now or what time shall we say?
Day after day,
Time is a constant,
So near and so far,
I want it to stop –
To cease to exist –
For time is a curse
Not an eternal bliss.

Together

Come with me,
Take my hand…
The journey of our lifetime awaits to begin,
I will guide you on a path of mind and of place,
One foot in front of the other,
A stride,
Sometimes a leap of faith,
Hold my hand…
I will never let you go,
The two of us on this journey,
So many places to go,
Our minds expanded,
Our souls enriched,
One word surmises all of this,
Love,
That word sums it up –
This journey we are on.

Tree

Stand tall and upright,
Stand tall and strong,
While you weather the storm,
Sway you must –
As the wind blows through you,
Until the calm comes,
So very old now,
But still so young,
Your limbs support life,
Give shelter and warmth,
For you are the mighty oak,
From the acorn were born.

Valentine

A kiss,
A cuddle,
The card and flowers are given
With a gift or three,
She smiles –
A genuine smile –
With a tear in her eye,
My love for her
Reaches the sky,
The only gift she really wants
From me on this valentine.

Will Power

A sudden yearning
Flows through me,
My body all a quiver,
Go on, do it!
You know you want to,
It keeps saying
Over and over,
The temptation –
So strong,
I push the yearning down,
Hoping
It will stay there,
But all of a sudden
It is back,
I take a deep breath
And out comes
A big sigh, o well,
I succumb to the yearning, and,
With a pop, the bag of crisps
Is open, I start to dig in,
Munching away,
My will power gone –

Left wanting –
Left shattered in my mind.

Winters' Morn

The clocks have gone back,
But still am up early,
Many clouds are about
Dulling the sky,
It may snow later,
Or it may now,
Even so the sky is a dark grey,
No sunlight can pierce it,
No warmth to be had
On this lonely grey day,
I close the door behind me,
Pull my coat tight around me,
BRR
That wind is chilly
As a cold draught sneaks in,
Winter is coming they say,
It's already here,
I think.